THE SYMPHONY OF TEARS AND HOPE

ANIKA SAHA

INDIA • SINGAPORE • MALAYSIA

ISBN 979-8-89066-730-4

Dedication

Dedicated to The GOD by whose grace I express my feelings, my younger sister Anushka who is my best friend, my parents & my grandparents.

"The Symphony of Tears & Hope" is a collection of poetry and prose about turmoils of teen age. About the experience of the lows, the highs, fear, love, loss, despair and teenage angst.

It is a collection of poems each with different emotions, with each poem dealing with a different mood swing of a teen. The book takes readers through a journey of the most bitter moments in life and finds sweetness in them -- because there is sweetness everywhere. If you are just willing to look though not everywhere it can be found.

A teenager's view of life when friends are not so close, parents are not too far, yet the world is an alien place. A desperate search of identity, a desire to fly yet wanting to be attached to the nest is all that this book is about.

Contents

About the Author

Anika is a sensitive teenager raised in Indian value system wanting to explore the world in her own impish ways. Somewhat scared, a little adventurous, a book worm to the core. She has a great sense of humor and can turn any tense situation into a happy one. In the most impressionable years of her life she expresses her emotions by writing poems. The poems reflect the emotions of a benevolent young girl.

She has an empathic heart and loves to treat other's problems as her own. Her deep understanding of fellow human being's frustrations, fears, despair has resulted in this collection of poems. Apart from writing poems she loves photography. Writing poems is how she deals with the trials & tribulations of her teenage life expressing her emotions.

Let the symphony begin & continue.....................

A Lapwing's Cry

Sorrowful, painful it cries out aloud,
All through the night,
Away from the crowd.

Moaning in despair,
The lonely lapwing flies by,
Away from the glare.

Like an outcast,
It flies through the night,
Trying to get away,
From the light.

Like a knife,
The cry slashes,
Through the night sky,
The cry flashes.

It sings of pain and ache abound,
And of the places,
Where joy can't be found,
Lonesome again, nothing to chase.

The lapwing will fly one last time,
Across the sky,
With the hope sublime,
Only to ask.... Why?

Glory

Oh! Glory,
On whose head do you shine?
Whose has been the story,
That's better than mine!

Glory, can't you be Mine?
I say thee.
And you climb the vine away,
Far away from me.

Why do you leave me?
Lonely and fore lone,
Why it is his head,
That you now adorn.

For you I walked the thorns,
For you I guarded the dawn,
For you I took the bull by the horns,
And finally it's you who scorns.

Fool! You say "Victory has passed away".
Though in pages of history you'll be buried,
It's your head,
That I've turned.

I've destroyed you and lead you astray,
Away, far away from love and joy,
Your greed has lead,
You into my sway.

To death I've lead you,
And you happen to be amongst the very few.
It makes me cold,
To see your death unfold.

In the end you might see,
With vengeance in your eyes you might ask,
What would it take,
To kill and destroy a cold soul like me.

But traveller know this,
You shall never find what you seek,
For I am bliss,
And you the abyss.

Fame

Fame!
You are just a wild horse untamed,
You lie and lead,
Unreal and on ego you feed.

It is our thoughts that you poison,
What to do with this treason,
That just defies all reason.

Ha! The crime is not mine,
But Thine.
The greed of yours abound,
Has taken you places,
Where sanity can't be found.

Kill me, if you will,
But free you won't be still,
Greed has consumed your soul,
Made it as black as coal.

For the pact you signed with greed,
On path of ruin must you tread,
Every moment,
With torment.

Love

It's jealousy in their minds that churns,
Tell me Dear Love,
How many minds will ye upturn?
In your treasure trove.

I am not to be blamed,
Yet still defamed.
Look around & you'll see,
It's envy whom you seek.

What you accuse me for,
Is not love.
For love is pure,
Not allure.

A feeling of the soul,
A silence to understand,
Listening the unspoken,
Together Forever.

A mirror corrupts

Gazing at the mirror,
To see if I am no inferior,
To match with those superiors,
And hide from those taunts & jeers.

I ask my reflection,
The right direction,
In that poisonous image,
I look for homage.

I look for solace,
In the wrong place.
I smile,
At the lies, all vile.

A mirror corrupts,
A mirror lies,
It breaks hearts,
Into shards apart,

Raging fires,
As time flies,
Destroying lives,
With it's lies.

My heart is mine

My heart is mine,
You may not deem it thine,
My heart belongs to me,
It will never belong to thee.

To me love does not creep,
It does not make me weep.
I am own master,
A cruel heartless monster.

My head does not bow,
This is my vow.
My heart is mine,
You may not deem it thine.

A chirp

What songs you sing?
What tales you bring?
What have you seen?
Where have you been?

O Little bird,
You quiver at your every word.
How excited must you be,
To tell all that you see.

You beat your wings,
All the while you sing.
Your chirps are symphonies,
Darling, sweet little stories.

From distant lands,
Through dust and sand.
You collect your wares,
Your sweet little stories to share.

I bow to GOD

I bow to GOD,
I do not know.
How to thank you, GOD?
For love and hope.

You have given me,
So much.
You've shown me,
Love, light and much.

You dried my tears,
Dispelled my fears.
To the light you lead,
Healed the wounds while I bled.

I do not know,
How to thank you GOD?
All I do is simply bow.
With folded hands,
I beg you forgiveness for it being so.

Child, I need no gold no silver,
Not at all not a sliver.
All I ask from your soul,
Your heart to be where gratitude starts.

Gash

The gash left on me,
Is a reminder for all to see.
The price paid,
For the wrong things said.

Where blood drips,
Defiance seeps.
To fight I seek,
No longer will I weep.

The pain of it,
Helps me beat.
Doubts and cowardice,
Vice and avarice.

I am stronger now,
No longer a coward now.
I'll fight till the end,
No longer break and bend.

My heart beats

My heart beats,
For all those who surround,
My family and friends.

My world is alight,
For I revel in their embrace,
Of my family and friends.

I smile,
To be with those whom I love,
My heart beats,
I've seized to weep.

I am free,
I've found my home.
Away from sorrow,
In their embrace.

Fallen

I've fallen times a many,
Broken to bone.
With a sorrowful symphony,
Sunk like a stone.

Hid from the glare,
Kept my pain unshared.
I cried and wept,
Hid from the darkness that crept.

No longer will I cry,
Never dismay, Never sigh.
My fall shall be the key,
A key that helps me see.

What I can be,
My destiny awaits me.
The power I wield,
No longer will I yield.

Torture

I inflict pain,
Quite insane.
Drive the knife,
As a respite from life.

This is a burden, I can't carry,
I quit, but I'm sorry.
My own anger scorches,
Burning like thousand torches.

I claw my own hand,
Bleeding in the sand.
Waiting for the end,
Wailing every moment.

Helpless, I torture myself,
With no one to bless.
To gain forgiveness,
To redeem myself.

Dread

How I dread,
My fate already said,
My path laid,
Trials and sufferings,
All ready and made.

In deep waters I wade,
My fate I can't evade,
Oh! how I dread,
The very things,
For which I was bred.

Oh! how this fight,
I must fight.
Why must I take part,
And perfectly play from the start.

May be it is my weakness,
That I cower before the darkness.
Cower before its suppress,
I shiver in my fate's embrace.

The world I knew

The world I knew,
Gave a splendid view.
Of green trees abound,
Of symphonies profound.

With nature galore,
Where birds did soar.
With waterfalls uproar,
The sea and the shore.

Yet a grey smoke was cast,
All was lost in the past.
Broken and marred,
Lost while I stared.

The world I knew,
Lost from view.
Never to find,
That scene left behind.

Sleepless nights

Tossing and turning,
Seeing the clock churning.
Desperately hoping,
To sleep and find healing.

Not a sound to hear,
Except my own anguish and fears.
When the world is still,
Horror and anguish is what I feel.

Scared of the darkness,
Scared of the loneliness.
In those sleepless nights,
The darkness must I fight.

Tired my eyelids flicker,
To find the light that glimmers.
Finally my fear fades away,
I fall into a slumber, in its sway.

Revenge

How I seethe in envy,
To see your moment of glory.
Why was I not up the pedestal,
Why was I the one who was to fall.?

What do you have that I do not?
Why do you shine and I not?
Why can't I bathe in glory and fame,
With everyone screaming my name.

I wish to avenge,
My defeat,
Seeking revenge,
Is ever so sweet.

Vengeance is sweet,
Yet justice must meet,
My folly,
An act so unholy.

It pulls me to grave,
In the dark hole,
It seems revenge did not save,
Farewell, my soul.

Living water flows on

Living waters flows on,
A song that goes on,
We sing of our mortal strife,
As we go on with our life.

We scream and wail,
Misfortune we hail,
Like those windy gales,
Who make our edifices crumble and fail.

Even when the world turns,
And time churns,
If we cry and despair,
Then our future will be broken and marred.

Living waters flow on,
A song that goes on,
No break no respite,
Of our wails inspite.

Wind

To your gentle breeze,
All trees yield with ease.
All firs and pine,
Bow to thine.

You bend all to your will,
All bow to you with reverence.
You move all that is still,
All look to you for guidance.

All bow to your glory,
To you kindness and your fury,
Your anger they fear,
Your friendship they hold dear.

A storm

A wind so savage,
Blows across the wreckage,
It calls for the storm to rage,
To let this war wage.

Dances the windy gales,
Plummeting the sails,
Accompanying the sailors wails,
The stormy passion it hails.

The waves break and plummet,
Accompanied with the rain so torrent,
They wreck the ships,
who drown as the water seeps.

The stormy sea swallows,
The ships and galleys hollow.
It leaves the surface barren and fallow,
The stormy passion ain't weak and shallow.

It's stormy passion wrecks,
It destroys and breaks,
It leaves destruction in its wake,
Nothing stands for none's sake.

Wound

I work harder than the rest,
With no respite, no rest,
Since the morning engaged,
In the eternal war so waged.

Even though I work all day all night,
Everyday getting ready to fight.
Still all laugh and reprimand,
My anguish they don't understand.

Their taunts hurt my soul,
It is charred as black as coal.
They wound me with pain,
They drive me insane.

No matter how hard I try,
To fly high,
Yet my wounded wings do not brave,
They break and pull me to grave.

The wound has left a scar,
A gash that leaves me marred.
No joy to see for miles afar,
Broken from taunts I heard so far.

The moonlit night

In the moonlit night,
In the soothing light,
Every petty raven,
Looks to thee,
And finds solace in thee.

You protect those who come to you,
Like drops of dew.
They flock to thee,
And find solace in thee.

Our thoughts that chase,
And leave us in a haze.
You bring peace,
To our minds left in unease.

All of our thoughts reside,
In your moonlit embrace.
In the moonlit field wide,
In You they find solace.

Starry messenger

Oh you twinkling stars!
You gaze afar,
What messages you bring,
Voices that walk upon your wings.

I gaze upon you,
At that starry view.
To gaze upon those constellations,
It brings me elation.

Gentle stories you tell,
Of warriors who fell,
Stories a many,
Strung up into a symphony.

You must have seen much,
That stories you tell as such,
For aeons you have seen,
Across the earth all that has been.

Starry messengers come again,
Along with the moon that wanes,
Your arrival I hail,
Come, come and tell me your tales.

Fathoms

What lies,
In the bottomless fathoms,
On the weary sea bottoms,
In the realm of the caverns.

What dwells,
Underneath the sea that churns,
What yearns,
To escape the darkness so swell.

Many songs have been sung,
With notes high strung,
How the lores' have told,
Of the secrets untold.

Our curiosities have woken,
To explore the darkness unspoken.
To find who smiles in her cavern,
Someone whom we cannot discern.

However chivalrous are we,
To travel across the waters uncharted,
In search of new things to see,
On this great blue sea.

Silence

Silence as it is,
The language of the wise.
Speaking much is an vice,
Of those fools so unwise.

Learned men know,
When to cock their bow.
When to speak,
To defend the weak.

The fools who clamour,
In search of glamour,
Speak never when necessary,
To them speech is an accessory.

In the silence unspoken,
Many a meanings are spoken.
The blabbering fools laugh and reprimand,
For the art of it they do not understand.

Silence ain't destitute and lonely,
The language of the saints,
Soft and homely,
Standing out when words won't.

Tales of Water

I shall stand by,
Underneath the sun so high.
On the water so transparent,
With the waves so opalescent.

The waves beat upon me,
Telling me the tales of the sea.
Tall tales a many,
Strung up into a symphony.

From the sailors so pale,
Who braved the gales.
To the affairs of the sea,
All come back to me.

I hear of distant lands afar,
And of the ships wrecked so far.
I see the mighty seas,
In your azure eyes.

For an ignorant boat like me,
Great fun it must be.
To hear more and more,
The tales of the sea evermore.

School

Why must I rise,
Everyday to be wise.
Sleepy I go to school,
This is not at all cool.

Spending hours a day on stuff so boring,
In school I go for learning.
I have to sit and learn,
Even though to play what I yearn.

Why must I study?
Why must I do my homework?
I wish to dance and play,
And spend my time away.

I cannot fathom,
Why can't I pay a ransom?
To be free,
From this wearisome task assigned to me.

Destiny

What does destiny behold,
Is it made of gold?
Or is it destitute and cold,
Worn out and old.

Will I soar?
Amongst the waterfalls uproar.
Or will I sink,
And weep upon the brink.

How will my life plan out,
Oh how I wish to find out.
Yet some things are better left hidden,
Never seen, forever forbidden.

It is best our paths are left untold,
Left darkened and cold,
It's GOD'S mercy to be so,
It gives us courage to traverse and go.

Best friend

Years ago I met a you,
When friendly soul were few.
With whom to walk abreast,
You were the one who understood me the best.

Together we laughed and played,
And danced with the tree that swayed.
We sang tunes a many,
Strung up into a mellifluous symphony.

You led me to the light,
When I had lost the fight.
You helped me stand,
My worth, she helped me understand.

The bond of ours,
Will never break, never cower.
Our friendship will stay,
Never break, never waylay.

Mortals

How puny are we mortals,
We think high.
And fill our lives with lies,
Thinking of us immortals.

We are made of flesh & bones,
Our skills we've learnt to hone.
Yet still we ain't immortals,
Just the puny little mortals.

We build our monuments so high,
A sight that meets the eye.
Something to remember us by,
For history to glorify our lies.

However we are just shadows and dust,
All that we built shall crumble to dust.
Our aspirations and lust,
Are nothing but dust.

Boasting our deeds,
Hiding misdeeds,
Forgetting GOD has made us,
Knowing GOD can finish us.

We do not understand,
That our edifices shan't stand,
They shall crumble no matter how tall,
Our pride shall shatter and fall.

Mustard Fields

In the little spring breeze,
Sways the mustard leaves.
The bright yellow sight,
Reflects the golden light.

The butterflies swarm,
Underneath the weather so warm,
The fields are stud,
With those golden buds,

It is a beacon of light,
In the darkness that shrouds.
A symbol of light,
For all in the crowd.

I'll run through the fields,
Where the light will be my shield.
Under that beautiful sunlight,
Away from that dark and weary night.

Maimed

To be tamed,
We must first be maimed,
No spirit shall be wild,
This I've learnt as a child.

A spirit unbroken,
Is a spirit unwoken.
To grow one must be broken,
Face pain, in order to be woken.

Wounds of toil,
Bind us to soil.
Work so bone breaking,
Cause our awakening.

Heard work shall teach,
And bring all within our reach.
Hard work maims,
It is what tames.

Grief Stricken

I am grief stricken,
That has let me weakened.
No more strength left,
Lost, while I wept.

Despair,
Has left me marred,
The pain unshared,
Has left me scared.

Grief has left me emaciated,
From joy I am parted,
I am now a shadow of my former self,
Residing in this dark and lonely hell.

Money

I have no money,
So can gain no sympathy,
No position no respect,
All this I already expect.

It is not that I want,
Fame and name abound.
However something still haunts,
The respect which can't be found.

I have no food, no home,
Have lived all my life alone.
I am starved,
The hunger has left me carved.

My fate was sealed,
For money I did not wield.
Even the nature does not shield,
The one who has already yield.

What a trifling thing it is,
Money is what it is,
Respect and love it brings,
It is what gives us wings.

Innocence

To know less,
Is to be blessed.
The virtue of innocence,
Is a bright little essence.

To know more,
Is to carry a burden so sore.
Of the darkness we possess no ignorance,
It drains away our innocence.

Innocence is bliss,
It lies far away from the abyss.
No grief to miss,
With the virtue of innocence as it is.

Fly Away

I want to fly away,
Into an unknown way.
Far far away,
To where happiness does lay.

With wings of dreams,
I want to fly away.
Amongst the sunlit beams,
Oh so far away!

It is a skirmish,
That leaves our heart tarnished,
Wild thoughts chase,
Me into this haze.

The mess is to much to cope,
Oh! how I hope.
To fly away,
Oh! so far away.

The mess is to much to handle,
Turned soon into a scandal,
I have no idea how to fix this mess,
No move for this chess.

I wish to fly away,
So far away,
To a woodland stream,
That dwells in my dreams.

Malice

Malice, O' Malice,
Are you an vice?
An accomplice,
Or simply nice.

Malice you are a poison ever so sweet,
The one created where ego and anger meet.
Green fire has moulded you stone,
You now belong in my bones.

You flow in my veins,
You've turned me vain,
You are a sharp sword to wield,
To heal wound that cannot be healed.

When the moon shone high,
And the hour was nigh.
You consumed my soul,
And made it as black as coal.

Yet I feel no regret,
How can I forget,
All those wounds left,
For whom I wept.

Those who left my soul tarnished,
Shall be punished,
I am consumed in evil,
Ready to cause a giant upheaval.

Weary Traveller

Desolate,
Disconsolate,
I alone roam,
On this road dark and forlorn.

I am an outcast,
Been cast away,
Afraid from the past,
I've lost my way.

All I seek tonight,
Is shelter from the weary night,
Then I shall leave,
Again, lost in the darkness that weaves.

Oh little lass, grant mercy!
That's all I ask of thee.
Grant me a shade at the best,
Where I can rest.

The Song Of Victory

Guitar strings strung,
A song so sung,
All youthful and young,
With blood and glory among.

A song of happiness,
Sung in the first light.
Notes of weariness,
After the war and the fight.

Victory was hard to come by,
Deaths and losses were never shy.
Yet a war is fought,
For our very beliefs and thoughts.

A triumphant victory,
Overshadows all misery.
All hail and sing,
The victory of their great king.

Who did I kill,
Who did I save,
With time thoughts might rest,
And weep off the sorrow off my breast.

Hide

I want to hide,
Shrunken from inside,
The world is wide,
In which I drown with full tide.

The world is cruel and harsh,
I do not have strength to last,
No courage to face,
The darkness that chased.

I want hide under my covers,
Underneath the soft light that hovers,
I want to dream of places,
Where smiles shall adorn all faces.

It is hard to go on,
And fight this evil so on,
The one that scorns,
And prickles me with thorns.

I wish to flee,
And find solace in thee.
I wish to forever hide,
And live on the other side.

My mind is my cage

My mind is my cage,
In a haze,
See how no mage,
Can free me.

My fears are my foe,
See how no one can sow,
The seeds of sympathy.

My sorrow is my death,
See how no wreath,
Can light up this grave.

My love is my light,
It gives me courage to fight,
This lonely battle of life.

My joy is my angel,
She shows me empathy,
Away from all misery.

Void

Oh! the light hurts my eye,
This I say with a sigh,
I know why,
Cause joy is a lie.

It is a void,
That I can't avoid,
It is a darkness that I cannot fight,
I cannot see no hope in sight.

In the darkness I dwell,
In the misery so swell,
This is my home,
This dark and lonely hell.

Pressure

Oh! the darkness is eating me away,
Why the life is so grey?
How did I ever come into your sway?

Oh! the pressure is too strong,
How could I ever do such a wrong,
And walk to death amongst the throng.

Oh! let the pain be gone,
Let bygones be bygones,
Oh! how I am the only one forgone.

This immense pain!
Please help me break the chains,
Yet I find I cry out in vain.

Now I understand,
This pain of mine,
Will not pass until I die,
Then let this be my last stand.

Death shall ease,
And bring my heart peace,
Close my eyes and lay,
Away far away from your sway.

Fear

Oh fear!
Why it is my soul you tear?
Why is it that you sear?
That pain in my mind.

Oh my sorrow!
It won't pass until the 'morrow,
Oh my ache!
It is joy I forsake.

Tell me dear,
Why it is that I fear,
And cry out thousands of tears,

Oh how I dream,
As I stitch amongst the seams,
To be free,
And to see the endless sea.

Oh my misery!
You are my enemy,
Stop will you not dear,
Until it is my soul that You tear.

The silent agony

Oh! how I'd love to be,
As happy as a lark,
Yet you'll see,
The difference as stark.

No hint of joy not love,
No hint of smile,
As I fight,
An evil so vile.

My joy is the darkness,
As I lay in its suppress,
None to help my sadness,
Oh! save me from this madness.

Oh! the silent agony,
Oh! the misery,
In a life so ordinary,
Why are you my enemy?

Oh! the silent agony,
Spare me some sympathy,
I am drowning in an endless sea,
For you to be or not to be.

Away from light

Sweet is the night,
And bitter the light,
Oh I give up!
Without a fight.

Cruel is the light,
And mercy the night,
Tell me what is the reason,
To fight.

Friend is the night,
And enemy the light,
Oh I quit!
This fight.

Oh I walk to you night!
Away from light,
Into your suppress,
Without a fight.

Abyss

To the edge of the abyss I say hello,
As I drown in an grief so mellow,
Darkness grips,
And makes me trip.

Into this shallow,
Bottomless pit below,
I walk to the edge of cliff,
As I trip and slip.

Oh the rush of air!
Is like heaven I swear,
Oh the darkness so pure,
Why do you bring me into this allure?

Oh I can't break away!
As I struggle in your sway,
Why do you waylay,
With all the lies that you say.

Oh! to this lone Ranger,
The darkness couldn't be stranger,
Alone I shall walk,
Amongst the devil's amok.

A raven's call

In the silence so melancholy,
That call is ever so unholy,
It is a omen that looms,
And foreshadows the call of doom.

Oh you raven!
In the graveyard you find your haven,
You are cursed to sing to the dead,
And fly amongst the graves undead.

You fly lime an outcast,
Sorrow in you thou hast,
Gone are the days of joy in the past,
In the graveyards you find,
Your refuge at last.

Little child,
It is not my fault that I mind,
But rather the eyes of humans so blind,
That cannot see the soul,
Lying across the colour behind.

Little lass!
It is not my destiny I rue,
Rather my due,
Left undued.

Not even a glance,
Or fair chance,
I was not given no love,
By none of you.

Words will flow

There is great beauty,
In the simplest of poetry,
Shielded from the mundane eyes,
Great beauty does lie.

It is hard to find,
The path to it ain't kind,
To see clear you musn't be blind,
To hear clear you must let your sorrow unwind.

It hides behind,
It is hard to find,
Even when it lies in plain sight,
It ain't for the blind.

If you look behind and see,
You'll find an endless sea,
Of touching poetry,
Of joy and sorrow in a symphony.

Like a trickle of water words will flow,
Like a glimmer of light words will glow,
To whom all heads will bow,
Words will set our heart aglow.

Thank you GOD

I thank GOD,
For my victory,
For all the glory,
For happiness in my story.

GOD helped me see,
What I could be,
GOD helped me see,
What potential hid in me.

Had it not been for GOD,
I would have been astray and lost,
Repenting mistakes of high cost,
Broken, in the cold frost.

GOD helped me be,
Who I am today,
Today all I want to say,
Is thank you GOD for all of that you have given me.

Expectations

Let me go,
Please I beg you.
Why do you hold me thus?
Why do you bind me in a truss?

What wrong have I caused you?
What ache did I give you?
That you condemn me to burn,
Why so? Why must I die for you?

Fool! I've done nothing,
Let me tell you something,
Look inside and tell me,
All the things around you that you see,
Wasn't it all what your heart seeked?

It was your greed and your envy,
That created this whirl,
Now you can do nothing but curl,
Up in your grave, around this constant swirl.

To death I submit

To death I walk with a trance,
Oh! isn't it a merry dance,
Lower my lance,
I give up without a chance.

Oh! I can't keep up this fight anymore,
As I drown in an grief without valour,
Look to light I can no more,
Oh! to death I soar.

Flying deep,
Into a sleep,
Close my eyes and weep,
No hope do I keep.

Oh! I quit,
As I walk on this road so unlit,
The end is near,
Yet I feel no fear.

Heart wrenching healing

Oh! I scream out loud,
With an grief so profound,
Healing there is none,
In an path that can't be undone.

Pain and ache abound,
Misery and grief surround,
Oh! I am in a place,
Where healing can't be found.

How to heal?
My heart so sealed.
I do not feel,
This joy so revealed.

This is a heart wrenching healing,
In time I am reeling,
My head is spinning,
Yet this sorrow is slowly leaving.

Time will heal,
Wake up and reveal,
This joy so sealed,
Which I cannot feel.

How will my heart heal?
And bring me joy so concealed,
Oh! my poor heart,
It has broken apart.

Sew up this wound,
On my heart,
That beats without a sound,
Bring me around,
To sorrow I shan't be bound.

This drug of time,
That grows on the vine,
It shall heal me,
It shall free me.

Silent tears

Silent tonight,
By the candlelight,
Flows the tears,
Of unduly fears.

In the silent night,
In the cold moonlight,
Flows those silent tears,
Of the pain so seared.

In the silent night,
By the firelight,
Flow those tears of sorrow,
A pain that won't pass until tomorrow.

These silent tears,
Are seared,
Into the night,
Away from the daylight.

Silent night

The peace is upon the air tonight,
In this clear silent night,
No cry no lament to be heard,
Nor the anguish of a bird.

The weary man tonight,
Shall rest his eyes and sleep,
No chance does he get to weep,
For work awaits him fortnight.

The city is at peace,
Yet darkness and pain go apiece,
Where has the sorrow gone,
Vanished from sight, forgone.

Labour and toil,
Of the day,
Has bound the man to soil,
As weariness creeps upon him,
In the many of ways.

This is life,
No time shall you get,
For sorrow and misery,
Rather it is the anguish,
That you must forget.

For there is labour
You can't waver,
And work to be done,
For this circle can't be undone.

Dandelions

I wish upon you,
As I bid you adieu,
A gentle breeze shall blow you away,
Take you away, so far away.
Into an unknown way.

You shall fly across,
Unknowing of what your path may cross,
Of your destiny you are uncertain,
Or path unknown.

Do you fear to be lost?
Do you know how much a mistake will cost?
How do you plan to find your way?
And to keep evil at bay.

I trust my instincts,
In the moonlight that glints,
The homely breeze,
Shall bring me peace.

Soon I shall find my haven,
And uncover my destiny so woven,
Till then I shall fly,
All through the night across the sky.

The words of GOD

In sorrow you think you sink,
However there are many who lie upon the brink,
Who weep,
As they delve into a sorrow so deep.

Your sorrow is nothing compared,
To the misery of those unshared,
Those who have no where,
Nor no one, nothing, all bare.

Look at those destitute and friendless,
Look at those homeless,
Look at those in eternal pain,
Or those driven insane.

Why do you curse?
Your life so worse,
Why can't you see the light?
When it is in plain sight?

You ungrateful wretch,
Your like is just like a sketch,
There are many who will clamour,
To live your life in full glamour.

Dispel

Let the darkness dispel,
Break this spell,
That shrouds all,
In its shadowy hall.

Let the darkness dispel,
Let hope, lighten.
The spirits of all who fell,
Let our, Lives brighten.

Come hope,
Come and make this your home.
Come and dispel,
Oh! please break this spell.

Please break our chains,
We are souls in pain.
Heal our hearts & dispel,
The darkness from our hearts,

Dry my tears

Someone please dry my tears,
Wipe them away,
Dispel my fears,
Please take them away.

Why is my face tear strained?
It has always been so stained.
My heart has always been so drained,
Love has always been in vain.

My heart still beats,
With a pain so sweet,
Sorrow is now my friend,
No longer a fiend.

Weakness

My body is so weak,
How vulnerable am I to weep,
It is easy to sleep,
And to hide in the shadows and weep.

To fight is foolish,
To indulge in such skirmish,
Best to hide,
And live on the other side.

This abyss is ever so wide,
That swallows me with full tide,
On which side does courage lie,
Why can't I find it, Oh why?

Pride

Pride, O Pride,
You blind my eye,
You make me evil,
And cause this giant upheaval.

This is my ignorance,
That has turned into arrogance,
I stand no chance,
To dodge this lance.

Why has my heart so turned?
And left me hurt and burned,
Why in my heart does envy churn?
Why in my heart does jealousy burn?

When will I learn,
That arrogance is a poison that burns,
Something that has changed my life,
And filled it with plenty strife.

In whose arms shall I find solace

In whose arms shall I find solace,
Whom shall I embrace?
To heal my heart,
That has broken apart.

Who shall caress my face?
Who shall wipe those tears off my face?
Who shall bring me peace?
And bring my heart ease.

Who can clear this haze?
That surrounds my face.
Who can show me light?
And give me courage to fight.

GOD I look to thee.
I find solace in thee.
Take me to that oblivion of mine,
I implore you through the mercy of Thine.

Freedom

Freedom, O freedom,
Come to my kingdom,
Walk with me,
I implore you to free me.

I am bound in chains,
Under the wreath so lain,
Under the power of those so vain,
Who drove me insane?

Come to me,
Hold my hand,
Befriend me,
Take me to a new land.

Break my cage,
Let this war wage,
This war has no age,
It was foreshadowed by the sage.

Oh mighty river!

From a sliver,
You began your journey,
Oh! mighty river,
You have carved your destiny.

Your fury so divine,
Have carved this ravine.
With fury your anger burst,
And turned everything in your way to dust.

Yet the gentle hand,
With which your waves does land,
Heals the heart,
Of those broken apart.

A long way you have come,
With this steady hum,
Now what does destiny hold,
For you who is made of gold.

Little human my journey is done,
This path can't be undone,
Now the oceanic waves I meet
Oh! to freedom I submit.

Heavy heart

Since Aeons it has grown,
With misery so more,
Seeds of ache so sown,
Have blossomed into trees, fully grown.

My heart is so heavy,
My soul it cannot carry,
My heart is on a frenzy,
With pain a plenty.

Oh this abysmal pain!
It brought me shame,
I cried out in vain,
To be rescued from this hurricane.

In the end, scattered across the land,
You shall find in the same,
The shards of my heart,
That has broken apart.

Beauty of the night

Behind the light,
Great beauty lies in sight,
Under the moon so white,
That shines ever so bright.

When the world is asleep,
And lies in the darkness so deep,
The gentle night comforts our sorrows,
And readies us for a bright tomorrow.

The gentle breeze,
That brings the trees ease,
In that Twilight field,
All of them do yield.

What power do you wield?
That from sorrow you shield,
Is it you smile,
That keeps away all things vile.

That moon so crescent,
That looks so opalescent,
All heads are bent,
To your mercy so relent.

The darkness adds to your splendor,
Enhancing your grandeur,
You are the night,
The one that shines more than light.

The lone soul in the night

Alone by the streetlight,
Stands a lone soul,
In the night,
Far away from the daylight.

In this cold moonless night,
You'll hear a lament tonight,
Of those sorrow so clandestine,
And of misery so viperine.

To walk alone he was cursed,
A curse he couldn't reverse,
Now in sorrow he must immerse,
Himself and traverse,
This lonely road all alone.

I had made a mistake,
And placed everything at stake.
To think that path to victory,
Lied without injury.

The folly of mine,
Is punished by thine.
I take it as a sign,
That with death I must dine.

Dancing in the rain

I've felt the pain,
Day after day it didn't wane,
I wish to forget,
And see the horizon where joy and sorrow met.

If my sorrow won't lessen,
And this burden won't lighten,
To the wind I shall sway,
And dance all my sorrow away.

I shall dance in the rain,
And let go of my pain,
Let go and fly away,
Let my sorrow wash away.

Crystal night

Oh, little birds!
Isn't it ever so fun,
To see this city so happy and gay,
Where all misery is forsake.

Alas, little human,
All is not meant for all,
We've seen things a many,
Of joy and sorrow in a symphony.

We've flown around,
Places of pain and ache abound,
Across streets round,
Where misery surrounds.

We've seen old men die without love,
We've seen starved children begging the streets,
We've seen many a women cry out hundreds of tears,
In tattered sheets.

They've hardened as leather,
Huddling together,
As they hide behind our feathers,
From this weary weather.

Their sorrow together,
Has turned this crystal night,
Into a sorrowful sight,
Far away from daylight.

Misty mountains

Far over the Misty mountains,
Flows the golden fountains,
A place with no pain,
Nor grief pertain.

A place of bliss,
Far away from the abyss,
No grief to miss,
Amongst the misty mountains as it is.

Free now to soar,
Amongst the waterfalls uproar,
This grief so sore,
I shall face no more.

Liar! This place is fake,
For joy is always forsake,
Never will one exist,
For never did one pre-exist.

Mercy of death

Death I embrace,
In you I find solace,
You clear up this haze,
That surrounds my face.

I do not think of you as a fiend,
Rather I wish to befriend,
On the bend,
Walk with you till the end.

You are not cruel,
As said in the lores,
Rather you give mercy,
And to joy you lure.

You heal those,
Suffering from eternal pain,
And those bodies,
In the graves so lain.

You bring peace,
To those destitute and friendless,
My mind is at ease,
To know, merciless thou art not.

I wish upon a Star!

I wish upon a Star,
That what shines afar,
Who are you?
That sees this great view.

Are you an angel of GOD?
Or are you the loved ones departed away,
Who can you be?
As you gaze upon this endless sea.

I am just one amongst the many,
Yet I sing you this symphony,
A plea for you to hear,
From near & dear.

Do nothing for me,
Please heed me,
There are many who need you,
Who are shielded from your view.

Heal them and bring them joy,
That's all I ask of you,
No trinket, no toy,
Just the mercy, the blessing of you.

Grey

Right and wrong,
Changes with time,
Like tunes of different songs,
Both mine and thine.

It ain't always black and white,
Even when in plain sight,
It all comes down to the eye,
Which sees the truth and the lie.

After all it is all grey,
A plain truth that does not waylay,
The perspective of ours,
Defines the sweet and the sour.

Little sister

With your dainty little poise,
And your sweet little voice,
You light up my door,
Since the clock struck four.

With no vice,
That smile of yours is an accomplice,
That mischievous little grin,
Removes all the sins.

Your innocence,
Is your arrogance,
To my pleas, your ignorance,
Is all but your innocence.

That little hug of yours,
Is nothing but allure,
I wish to hug you tight,
And see you in plain sight.

Astray

I want to stay,
Yet I've lost my way.
Gone astray,
So far away.

I am waylaid,
Into this unknown sway,
The evil no longer at bay,
What is left for me to say.

How many hearts have I broken,
With words unspoken,
With my choice,
That I couldn't voice.

How did I break my vow?
And cause such sins to sow,
How could I sink so low,
And let my head bow.

Now my heart is torn,
With broken promises so sworn,
In the darkness I am forlorn,
Without hopes to be reborn.

Temptation

Temptation,
Soon it grows into addiction,
What a word,
It is entirely absurd.

What a sweet little thing,
Temporary elation it brings,
It ain't bitter,
It just keeps getting sweeter.

Yet if this continues,
My fate I shall rue,
Temptation is a vice,
Filled with malice.

It destroys and kills,
It destroys until,
I am nothing but a mere,
Shadow of fear.

The wheel of time

The wheel of time,
Is like a drug of wine,
We think to procrastinate,
Swimming into its bait.

We've learned to wait,
Continuing things in our merry gait,
We've learnt to hate,
Things which cannot be late.

One might say that it is haste,
That makes waste,
But is it true,
Or just our notions untrue.

So deep have we sunk into this addiction,
That procrastination,
Is now more than a temptation,
A drug that brings us elation.

But as the wheel of the time churns,

The delay in our heart does burn,

Forever those chimes,

Shall remain lost in time.

The song of silence

The song of silence,
Is beautiful to the ear,
Those destitute tunes,
Are beautiful to hear.

I wish to live alone,
In the shadows,
Away from the light that shone,
Underneath the hallows.

I wish to live,
Far away from the trouble that weaves,
In the silent night,
Away from the harsh daylight.

To live alone,
Is to achieve freedom,
A victory so won,
In my own little kingdom.

The song of silence,
Is a soulful song.
A song for which I long,
A longing ever so strong.

I wish to listen,
And let my sorrow lessen,
Oh thus song of silence,
My life you shall lighten.

Arrogance

Arrogance,
You are a vice,
Ignorance,
Is your accomplice.

I've become proud,
Setting myself apart from the crowd,
It is my ego,
That I cannot forego.

Pride,
It is an abyss so wide,
It spits poison in my mind,
That turns me blind.

Now I am waylaid,
As I struggle in your sway,
Arrogance is no longer at bay,
It seems I've lost my way.

How did I turn,
Why this poison do I yearn?
How did I change?
With this act of revenge.

Time flows

Living waters flow on,
A song that goes on,
A song of time,
Till the end of time.

Like the flow of rivers,
Our lives go by like slivers,
They flow from our hands,
Like those particles of sand.

No break no respite,
No stop In spite,
Our petty whims,
Those that wish to win.

Our whims a many,
Impairs us to this symphony,
A song that goes on,
Living waters flow on.

Destitute

Alone and lonely,
With the darkness unfriendly,
Alone I dwell,
In my little dark hell.

Destitute and friendless,
Knee deep in loneliness,
All sad and cold,
Been so of old.

What does friendship say,
Is it a path or just waylay,
What does love portray,
Is it pure or just dismay.

Once love broke my heart,
Will it break it again apart,
I cannot face the pain,
Once more once again.

Its best to dwell,
In my own little hell,
Alone and lonely,
All destitute and unfriendly.

Truest friends

I thought I was cursed,
To walk on this road so worse,
Yet I found three more souls immersed,
Ordered with me to traverse.

They held me up all night,
And showed me the light,
They hugged me tight,
And gave me courage to fight.

They danced with me,
They sang with me,
And made the one of the truest three.

They helped me see,
What I could be,
What life has in store,
All golden and evermore.

Even if with storm or fireball,
The world must fall, we shall brave it all,
Our friendship shall last,
With our memories from the past.

Golden dreams

When we sleep, our dreams and aspirations,
Weaved with imagination,
Our own little creations,
Factors of jubilation.

In deepest sleep,
Great hope do we keep,
Of future so bright,
Bathed In sunlight.

Our dreams are made of gold,
Not broken nor old,
A joyous essence,
We laugh in its presence.

Great joys it brings,
It is what gives us wings,
To the fly to the highest of heights,
To win the greatest of fights.

Hold my hand

GOD! please hold my hand,
As I wander across the land,
Grant mercy,
To a weary traveler like me.

I am lost, I know,
I am knee deep in woe,
GOD help me,
Oh I beg to thee!

I do not know,
Which way to go,
I am alone in these dark woods,
The darkness is darker than it ever would.

To whom shall I confess,
My sorrow so repressed,
GOD hear me,
Please GOD help me.

GOD I am lost,
I've made mistakes of high cost,
All I ask of you GOD,
Is to let me find solace in thee,
In the arms of thee.

Broken dreams

One thinks to fly high,
Soaring across the sky,
To dream High,
To see life with no lie.

However if truth be told,
Life is way more cold,
It has been so of old,
With secrets untold.

To dream big is a sin,
To whom nobody can win,
For reality stands apart,
From the dreams that break your heart.

Dreams shatter,
As if they do not matter,
Our hearts shatter,
Across the land the scatter.

Dreams are just lies,
Told to brighten our lives,
But one day they shall break,
With that profound ache.

Poison

Poison in our hearts,
It breaks us apart,
Unaware are we of its existence,
Yet it still diminishes us with persistence.

Envy and jealousy seethe,
In the air we breathe,
It breaks us apart,
And leaves a gash instead of a heart.

We are it's slave,
Each and every knave,
We bow to it with good will,
Unknowing of its desire to kill.

We submit to it,
Just to sit on the highest seat,
To wear the crown,
And laugh while everyone frowns.

Yet poison will kill us from inside,
Bring us over to the dark side,
We shall exist in a world of no love,
No hope in the trove,
Nowhere to hide.

To accept

Oh, where was I!
I used to fly high,
Bathed in fame and glory,
Burned into history.

Now look where I dwell,
In this darkened hell,
From the fallen wounds I've bled,
No longer the crown on my head.

Defeat I must accept,
My fate took a turn, I didn't expect,
How can I accept,
My fate's new aspect.

How can I look,
At the direction my destiny took?
How can I agree,
To the change of 180 degrees.

Ignorance is bliss,
Yet it leads me to the abyss,
It seems ruefully I shall accept,
My cold and destitute new aspect.

Addiction

Oh addiction!
My sweet temptation,
You bring elation,
Yet are an delusion.

You spit poison in my mind,
Which leaves me hurt and blind,
You are poisonous, addiction,
You drown me in your illusion.

I wish to break free,
Find shore in your poisonous sea,
You liar you knave,
Or else you shall pull me to grave.

Solo

To fly high,
I need to walk alone,
Fly solo,
Or sink like a stone.

Alone all alone,
I can let my skills hone.
Solo, I can fly,
To the highest of skies.

To a lone lone Ranger,
The darkness ain't stranger,
For he has met the dark heart of his,
That seeks to fly solo with joy amiss.

Silent angel

Silently you tread,
Gently upon the weeds,
At the pitiful sight you gaze,
And lessen the pain with your grace.

You come softly to ease,
All the souls left in unease,
Yet you ask for no repay,
Even from those who betray.
Your smile is all I need, you say.

You smile as you see,
That joyous melee,
Then turn and walk,,
And disappear amongst the chaos amok.

You were an angel so silent,
That came and went,
You broke the chains,
Of our abysmal pain.

Yet no trace to find.
You left behind.
Broken & frail,
We the mortals forever fail.

Mistake

If in our journey,
In our path to victory,
Lies no break, no injury.

Then the path of ours is wrong,
Life ain't a flawless song,
Mistakes come and go,
This we cannot forego.

Our mistakes and faults,
Our progress they do not halt,
They prune and teach,
And bring all within our reach.

Only when we fall and tumble,
Only when we break and crumble,
Do we learn to stand tall,
Strengthened from our fall.

Broken heart

You broke my heart,
Broken into pieces apart,
Then it was cast away,
Left to rot in the darkness that sways.

It is not love,
That sweet little dove,
But a drug that does not save,
And pulls you to grave.

Love ain't sweet,
But a bitter treat,
Sweet while it lasts,
Then leaves a dark, broken past.

Your heart it will always break,
Let joy be always forsake,
Love ain't sweet and pure,
Just a temptation, an allure.

Dawn

In the darkest of nights,
Glimmers of light creep,
Hope seeps,
To all those who weep.

Dawn arises,
Everyday the sun rises,
Burning away the cold,
It's done so of old.

The golden sunlight,
Triumphs the darkened night,
Across the vestiges of fight,
It brings hope with all its might.

From its ashes it comes again,
Washing away all pain,
Like a phoenix it soars high,
Up and above into the sky.

Sisters' love

To me my sisters,
Though they always pester,
Holds the utmost importance,
Their life weighs more than mine.

I shall love them,
Till the ends of the earth,
I shall sacrifice myself,
For their little smiles.

Whatever my life's worth,
My sisters are worth more,
I'll do anything for them.

For I love them,
More than anyone,
Or anything else in the world,
My heart beats for them.

Scar

It is a scar,
That has left me marred,
I am hurt and wounded,
To sorrow, I am bounded.

The trials that I've faced,
Has left poison in my mind so laced,
My heart has been pierced,
With a pain so fierce.

The aches that I've faced,
Has left me broken and wounded,
A wound that can't be mended,
I am left hurt and scared.

The gash left on me,
Has left me unable to see,
This blinding pain,
Has driven me insane.

This angry weal,
That can't be healed,
My fate is sealed,
I've already let myself yield.

Why fight, writhe in pain?
When I must get hurt again.
I am already under the ache so vain,
My heart asks, "why must I fight
again"?

Blood, sweat and tears

Blood sweat and tears,
Is all I've got,
Toil and fears,
I haven't forgot.

Blood is split,
From the wounds I got,
Got under the pain so built,
Yet the ache I never forgot.

Years later,
I am stronger,
The ache's better,
Now I am molded harder.

Sweat flows free,
It tires me,
To continue,
My fate I rue.

Today as I sit upon my throne,
And enjoy my victory so won,
I thank the toil so spent,
In the years that went.

Tears so cried,
Up in the night so wide,
In the moonlight,
Before my last fight.

Now war is done,
Victory I've won,
Tears so crystalline,
Brought me on top of the vine.

Blood, sweat and tears I've spilt,
Yet they do not let me wilt,
It keeps away the guilt,
As I look at my life so built.

Childhood

Childhood, my sweetest memory,
A distant story,
Enveloped in gold,
Are those memories of old.

Years ago when I was a child,
All ignorant and wild,
A spoilt brat was I,
Running across the hill so high.

Dancing underneath the rain,
Feeling no pain,
I made friends with the sun,
Feeling everything a victory so won.

A joyous smile,
Kept away all things vile,
I never knew of the abyss,
To me ignorance was bliss.

However the sands of time churned,
Much now I've learned,
Past is past,
Nothing forever lasts.

How sweet is this symphony,
My distant memories in a cacophony,
That far fetched story,
Lost in the pages of history.

Lost

(Dedicated to the accident victims. To the snatches of poetry
of a lost poet…)

Your soul is lost,
So is your body,
Amongst the mangled remains,
You are lost.

I know you not by your name,
Nor your breeding,
But by your pieces of poetry,
Found upon the ground.

You touched my heart,
Even when you were long gone,
With your touching pieces of poetry,
You left a lasting impression on me.

Alas! Such a great poet,
Was fated to be lost,
No trace left,
You are forever lost.

I look to the stars and ask,
Who was it for,
Who wrote the sublime notes,
Such great poems and quotes.

I look to the stars,
And find one twinkling afar,
I look up and gaze,
To see the heaven brightened by your grace.

Shame

Death is my solace,
I look to it through a haze,
Misery surrounds my face,
Find you will of joy no trace.

Heavy is this pain,
That drives me insane,
I hoped in vain,
To find someone to blame.

The blood rushes in my veins,
As I try to fight this hurricane,
Yet I find my body in drain,
And my name in stain.

Now I have no name,
Bound I am in chains,
Of this abysmal shame,
That drives me insane.

I look to flee,
And find solace in thee,
Today heal me,
I implore you to free me.

Lament

A lament of sorrow I sing,
A pain in my heart does string,
This abysmal pain,
It will drive me insane.

Oh! How cruel is this world,
Why curses at me do you hurl,
Why do you laugh at my misery,
And spare me no sympathy.

Oh happiness is a delusion!
I am drowning in this illusion,
Somebody please give me a solution,
Some resolution.

To heal my heart,
That Is breaking apart.
Each moment,
With your torment.

The children of GOD

We are the children of GOD,
You and me,
Maybe we cannot see,
But GOD holds us dear both you and me.

GOD protects us all,
all those who tumble and fall,
GOD brings them to the light,
GOD gives them courage to fight.

We all dwell in GOD'S mercy,
Yet we cannot see,
All that we are given,
We take for granted, the times we're forgiven.

Yet still GOD loves all,
All the children in his hall,
God shields all those who fall,
God gives us love, much more and all.

Your grey shadow

(I dedicate this poem to all those who have passed away)

Where shall I find you,
You are gone,
No trace of yours left, forgone.

Your voice with the wind,
Your body with the fire,
And your ashes with the river, all gone.

Where shall I find you,
On this earth,
Can I ever see you,
Again by the hearth.

You are now,
Only but a memory,
A moment engraved in time,
In time nothing is left behind.

You have walked away,
So far away,
Your shadow will stay,
With the ones you've left away.

Not a day goes by,
That I don't cry,
Oh you grey shadow!
Finally it was joy you foreshadowed.

Delirium

I am in a delirium,
The one that belongs to an asylum,
I am no longer sane,
Yet I scream out in vain.

My thoughts are a mess,
I am unable to confess,
This sorrow so repressed,
That has turned me into a mess.

This sorrow drove me mad,
And left me ever so sad,
Endless Despair,
You, I've learnt to fear.

You tortured me,
With those sleepless nights you chased me,
You spared me no sympathy,
You did not see,
The soul in me.

I've gone crazy,
With pain a plenty,
My heart is empty,
Lost to your vanity.

Soaring High

To the eagle eye,
That soars so high,
The world appears small,
Nothing so fearsome, oh! none at all.

Oh how it would feel!
To soar through the clouds, concealed,
To look at the world below,
To see men engrossed in their works so mellow.

To that little sparrow,
Great fun it must be,
To fly above and see,
The affairs of this city.

Oh! how I would love,
To fly above,
Ever so high,
Across the sky.

A little sparrow

Soaring the skies,
I see with a sigh,
A little sparrow,
Flying ever so high.

It knows not,
Of its fate so fraught,
It knows not,
That to death he is brought.

It flies by,
Up & down the sky,
With equal joy,
Across the sky.

With each beat of his wings,
A song in my heart does string,
Oh! You poor sparrow,
Your future is ever so harrow.

It's however GOD'S mercy,
That it's future it cannot see,
For the lamb shall lick its butcher's hand,
Unknowing of where his head is to land.

Behind the colour

With a raven's call,
The world shall stall,
With that piercing call,
The world shall fall.

No longer in the shadows,
Shall we dwell,
Rather we shall unleash,
Complete hell.

We've been outcasts,
For long,
Now we shall let our pasts go past,
And sing this weary song.

It's our battle cry,
That soars so high,
Bound in chains, we shall be no more,
Free now shall we be to soar.

In the end when you shall ask me why,
I shall judge you with no mercy,
Yet I shall tell you no lie,
It was your blind eye,
That couldn't see,
The soul behind the colour of me.

Sand castles

My sand castle,
A dream envisioned,
A glowing vision,
My castle of oblivion.

By the roaring sea,
You stood to be,
I built you with love,
You rose high above.

To your ballista, your towers,
The hardened souls did cower,
My dreams wove,
Your place in the cove.

What a pretty sight were thee,
As you stood by the endless sea,
I thought you'll stand,
For eternity on the sand.

But you too broke away,
Fell to the roaring bay,
The waves washed you away,
Unspoken, broken, Oh So far away!

Confinement

The bars of steel,
My spirit they seal,
Youth and happiness they steal,
Distraught, dismay they reveal.

They are made,
To punish.
Can never evade,
Lives they tarnish.

In name of justice,
In name of peace,
Men are imprisoned,
Forced to dwell in this cold darkened prison.

Golden ever glowing dreams,
Days underneath the sun beams,
Lost and forlorn,
Caged in these walls of thorns.

Across the bars,
Light shines afar,
Birds fly free,
Their freedom I envy.

In the solitary walls confined,
In the darkness undefined,
I pray to find,
Eternal peace of mind,
Engraved in time,
All that I left behind.

Warriors

I am a soldier,
I dwell in the frontiers,
I possess no fear,
My Anthem is all I hear.

Farewell! I must leave,
This burden I must heave,
For duty calls,
For our courage, our souls, our all.

Good bye!
I shan't lie,
I may return or may not,
My future be sweet or be fraught.

I'm proud to say,
All price I pay,
My life, my soul,
I commit to you, whole.

A warrior as I,
Can never break, never cry,
For when motherland calls,
Ready to die, one and all.

Anika Saha | 181

Forgive me

I've hurt you,
Refused you your due.
Unwoken, unspoken,
Promises all broken.

I have no right,
To ask for mercy and light,
To beg for forgiveness,
Sorry for this mess.

You are not obliged,
To spare amnesty,
For I have lied,
For which I am guilty.

I have no right to look into your eyes,
For I have lied grave lies,
Yet I am dying to earn your forgiveness,
To redeem myself to thyself.

Mercy,
Amnesty,
Forgive my crimes,
One last time..

The new dawn,
The journey of teenage,
The changing of body,
Of Mind & moods
Where friends are not so close,
Where parents are near yet far,
The pressure to perform
The despair , the independence,
The dependence and ignorance,
The fitting in or may be not,
The anger, the jest,
The love, the heartbreaks,
My journey, thru the thoughts,
In poems that's all I present,
The symphony of tears & hope.

Anika Saha